Weather

Library of Congress Number: 87-28715

2 3 4 5 6 7 8 9 0   91 90 89 88

Printed and bound in the United States of America.

Library of Congress Cataloging in Publication Data

Weather.

(Science and its secrets)
Includes index.
Summary: Examines cloud formations, weather patterns,
trade winds, forecasting methods, and various factors which
contribute to unique weather patterns in various parts of the
world.
1. Weather—Juvenile literature. 2. Meteorology—
Juvenile literature. [1. Weather. 2. Meteorology]
I. Series.
QC981.3.W42   1988   551.5   87-28715
ISBN 0-8172-3079-3 (lib. bdg.)
ISBN 0-8172-3096-3 (softcover)

WEATHER

Raintree Publishers — Milwaukee

Contents

The Seasons

Why don't people go to the beach in December? 8

Is it cold everywhere in America in December? 9

Why is it hot in the summer? 10

How does the sun warm the earth? 11

Why can't the sun be seen at night? 12

Why doesn't the sun warm the earth very much in winter? 13

What happens between two January firsts? 14

The Water

Where in space is the earth? 16

What is between the sun and the earth? 16

What is a good way to describe the earth? 17

Why is the sky blue? 20

Why does a street dry up after a rainfall? 21

What is the water cycle? 22

Why do clouds float in the sky? 24

Why is it hard to see in the fog? 24

How much does a cloud weigh? 25

Why do clouds move? 25

The Climates

What is the proper way to dress for winter? 28

Why are climates so different? 30

How is *climate* defined? 32

What is a polar climate? 33

What is the best example of a temperate country? 34

Is a Mediterranean climate limited to the Mediterranean? 35

What is a subtropical climate? 36

What is a tropical climate? 37

Where can an equatorial climate be found? 38

The Unpredictable Weather

How is rain formed? 40

Where does a rainbow get its colors? 41

Is it raining or snowing? 42

Why does hail cause damage? 42

Why does a thunderstorm occur? 43

Why does a thunderstorm make so much noise? 43

Where does lightning originate? 44

What is a storm? 45

What is a tornado? 48

What is a monsoon? 49

What is a blizzard? 50

What is a cyclone? 50

The Weather

How is meteorological information obtained? 52

How is meteorological information used? 54

Of what use is a weather report? 55

Can anyone be a meteorologist? 57

Why are there errors in weather predictions? 57

Can pollution change the weather? 59

Can people change the weather? 61

Glossary 62

Index 64

THE SEASONS

Why don't people go to the beach in December?

In most of the Northern Hemisphere, swimming in an ocean in December is uncomfortable. The water is cold at that time of year. Since summer, the water has lost much of its warmth. The sun now hardly warms the water at all. It is low on the horizon, and days are short. This is winter; it is cold. The sky is often overcast with clouds. Snow or cold rain falls. Sometimes the wind is intense. Weather conditions at the beach are not favorable. The weather does not encourage swimming.

Taking a shower in summer is often a necessity and not only for cleanliness. The weather is hot. The human body, which is not accustomed to the heat, does not tolerate it well. A shower lowers body temperature. For the same reason, humans normally eat cold foods at this time of the year.

In winter, the opposite is true. Drinking hot beverages and eating hot foods help combat cold temperatures. It is all a question of balance. Taking a cold shower in winter lowers body temperature at a time when it is more difficult to get it back up again. Under certain circumstances, lowering body temperature could be dangerous.

In winter, chestnut vendors replace ice cream vendors.

Is it cold everywhere in America in December?

No. Along the Pacific Ocean, temperatures are moderate and little if any snow falls, except in the mountains. The same is true of numerous desert regions of the Southwest. In Hawaii, of course, temperatures are high, and no snow falls the year around. Snow seldom falls in Florida, and December temperatures are moderate. In the lower South, chilling rains fall, but as a rule temperatures remain above freezing.

The Pacific Ocean causes the moderate weather along its coast. Hawaii lies within the tropics, where the weather is always warm. Florida lies near the tropics. The warm Gulf of Mexico influences weather in the lower South.

In the East and the Midwest, in the mountainous regions of the West, and on the Great Plains, the picture in December is different. The days are chilly, if not freezing cold. The earth is frozen, and ponds and streams are iced over. This cold comes from the Arctic by way of Canada.

Why is it hot in the summer?

In summer in the Northern Hemisphere, the sun is high in the sky and shines much of each day. The days are long. The ever-present sun explains the summer's heat. One proof of this lies in the fact that if a cloud passes in front of the sun, the temperature suddenly drops.

The sun is a star just like the ones seen in the sky at night. And there are more stars in the universe than grains of sand on the biggest beach of the world. Like the earth, the sun is a ball, but much larger. The diameter of the sun is 868,000 miles (1,400,000 kilometers). That of the earth is 7,900 miles (12,760 km). Thus, the diameter of the sun is more than one hundred times greater than the earth's. The surface of the sun reaches a temperature of about 10,000°F (5,500°C). Its center is about 27,000,000°F (15,000,000°C). As a matter of fact, the sun is a giant nuclear bomb that continues to explode. It has been in existence for more than five billion years and will last again as long.

Nevertheless, the sun is a small star. It exists in a universe of suns.

Summer solstice: June 21

Spring equinox: March 21

Autumn equinox: September 21

Winter solstice: December 21

East (sunrise)

West (sunset)

| 12 midnight | 2 a.m. | 4 a.m. | 6 a.m. | 8 a.m. | 10 a.m. | 12 noon | 2 p.m. | 4 p.m. | 6 p.m. | 8 p.m. | 10 p.m. | 12 midnight |

Solar time

| 2 a.m. | 4 a.m. | 6 a.m. | 8 a.m. | 10 a.m. | 12 noon | 2 p.m. | 4 p.m. | 6 p.m. | 8 p.m. | 10 p.m. | 12 midnight | 2 a.m. |

Summer time

This illustration shows the apparent path of the sun in the sky at the time of the winter solstice, the spring and autumn equinoxes, and the summer solstice. A *solstice* is the sun's direction in space when it appears at its farthest point north or south among the stars. An *equinox* is either of the two times each year when the sun crosses the equator and day and night are of equal length. It is easy to understand why the sun warms the Northern Hemisphere more in summer than in winter. Not only is its path longer, but it is also much higher above the horizon.

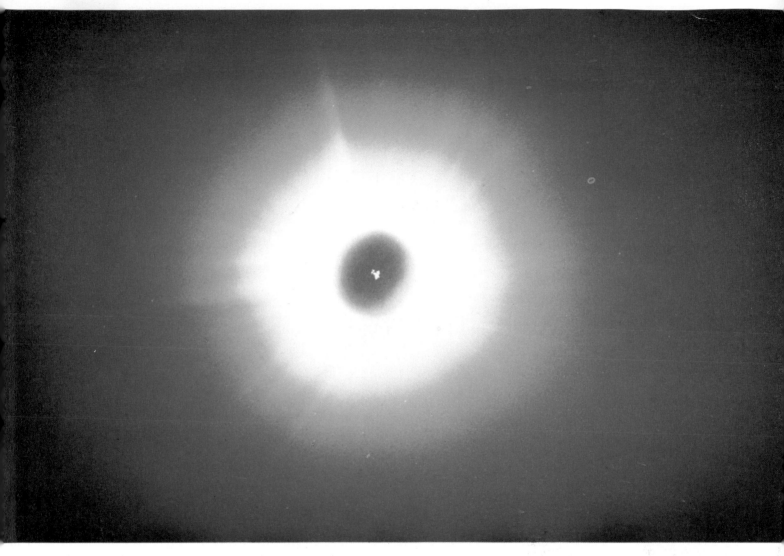

How does the sun warm the earth?

The sun is a sort of giant nuclear bomb which is constantly exploding. It sends its light and heat in all directions in the form of radiation. It acts like a fire. Near the sun, the radiation is intense and the heat is unbearable. A rocket sent to the sun would never reach its surface. The rocket would turn to ash millions of miles before it could get there.

This immense radiator is dangerous, and so are its rays. But fortunately, as they move away from the sun, solar rays lose a large portion of their energy. Their strength decreases. When they arrive on earth, they have traveled 93 million miles (150 million km). They are then bearable. If the earth were closer to the sun, everything would burn. If it were located a bit farther away, everything would freeze. As a matter of fact, the earth's environment is the result of the planet's position with respect to the sun.

Moreover, before the sun's rays strike the earth, they are filtered by the atmosphere. The atmosphere is the envelope of gas that surrounds the earth. The sun's rays become moderate, but they still provide warmth and energy.

This eclipse of the sun was photographed in Mexico on March 7, 1970.
Below is a cross-sectional view of the sun.

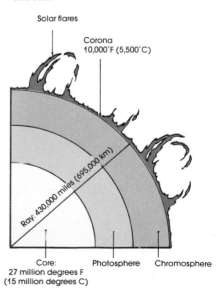

Solar flares

Corona
10,000°F (5,500°C)

Ray: 430,000 miles (695,000 km)

Core:
27 million degrees F
(15 million degrees C)

Photosphere

Chromosphere

Why can't the sun be seen at night?

During the day, even when the sky is overcast, no one doubts that the sun is present. For one thing, there is a certain degree of daylight. For another, a break in the clouds might reveal the sun. And anyone in an airplane above the clouds on an overcast day would see the sun.

On days when nothing hides the sun, a person can see that it always rises from the same direction—the east. It disappears from view in the opposite direction—the west. People of long ago used these facts to deduce that the sun revolves around the earth in one day. Everyone now knows that this is not true. The earth revolves around the sun in 365 days. But to explain day and night, one must know that the earth rotates on its polar axis, with one side facing the sun—that is day; and one side facing away from the sun— that is night.

The earth rotates completely in twenty-four hours, while revolving around the sun in one year. It is sort of like a spinning top turning around a lighted lamp.

If the earth did not rotate, the side exposed to the sun would burn. The other side would freeze. But it does turn, regularly and rather quickly. No part has time to burn or freeze.

These four photographs were taken from a satellite that remained stationary with respect to the earth. They show the rotation of the planet. India is shown between noon and toward the end of the day.

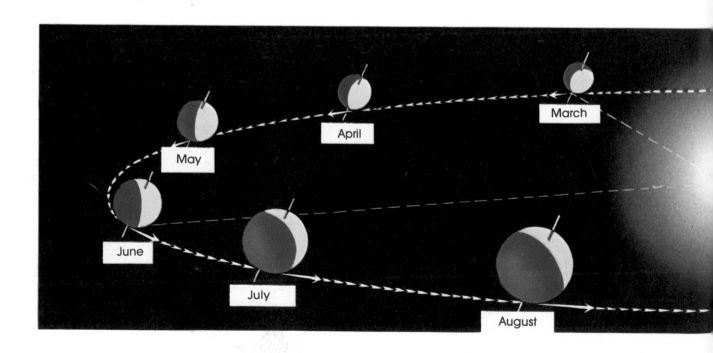

March
April
May
June
July
August

12

Why doesn't the sun warm the earth very much in winter?

December 21, daytime in the United States. Close to the North Pole, the sun has not appeared for three months, but it has been shining without interruption for three months at the South Pole. Notice that when it is day over the continental United States, it is night over Europe and part of the Altantic Ocean.

The large orbit of the earth around the sun. During the course of a year, because it is inclined on its polar axis, the earth does not always face the sun at the same angle.

The earth rotates continually during a twenty-four hour period. It completes its journey around the sun in one year. The distance from the sun to the earth varies little during the year. The energy the earth receives from the sun's rays is, therefore, almost always the same. Why, then, does the winter sun seem cooler than the summer sun? The reason is that the earth is at an angle to the sun on its path around it. In other words, a given region of the earth faces the sun at a certain angle, depending on the season of the year.

In summer, the United States faces the sun more directly. The rays approach a 90° angle to the earth, and the sun supplies a maximum of energy. In contrast in winter, the angle of the rays is lower. So, then, is their intensity.

In addition, the duration of the presence of the sun, and, therefore, the supply of heat, is short in winter —eight hours on December 21. It is much longer in summer—sixteen hours on June 21.

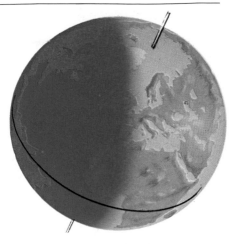

June 21, nighttime in the United States. In the regions neighboring the North Pole, the sun will not set. But in contrast, the night is not interrupted around the South Pole. Here day has come to Europe and to Africa.

The sun is not stationary. It moves at a speed of 536,000 miles (864,000 km) per hour around the center of a group of stars that together form what is called a galaxy. The galaxy is also on the move. Everything is in motion in the universe.

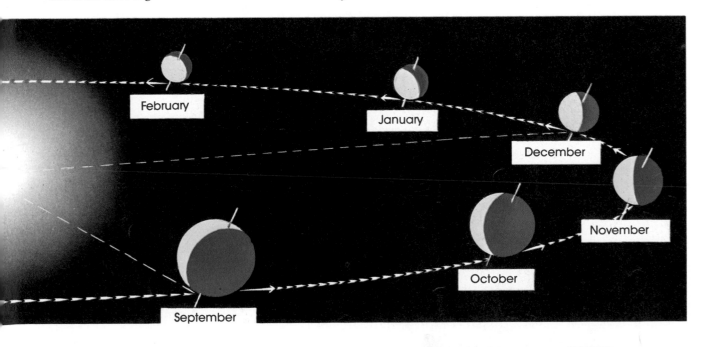

February

January

December

November

October

September

What happens between two January firsts?

On January 1, every year without fail, the earth and the sun are in the same position with respect to each other. However, the earth travels around the sun. Its positions on December 31 and on January 2 are not the same as on January 1. As days pass, the Northern Hemisphere will be more inclined toward the sun, and more heat will be added to it. As the rays become more and more direct, temperatures will rise. Before a year passes, though, the radiation of the sun again becomes less direct and temperatures fall.

Temperature changes month after month. Major changes are called the seasons. Start with January 1. It is cold, for this is winter. Then, in April, warmth comes back little by little. It is spring. In the month of June, hot weather arrives. It is summer. Then the temperature begins to sink again. Fall has come.

The winter solstice starts on December 21 and ends on March 20. The spring equinox begins on March 21 and ends on June 20. Summer— the summer solstice—starts on June 21 and ends on September 20. The fall, or autumn equinox, begins on September 21 and ends on December 20.

During winter, the nights are long. Cold temperatures prevail. There is cold rain, more often snow. The trees are bare. There are no flowers in the countryside. This is the season when it feels good to come home. But it is also the time for snowballs, skating, and skiing.

In spring, which starts on March 21, nature comes alive. The days get longer, and the temperature becomes milder. The sun shines more often although heavy rain showers or hail are common. On trees, buds form and blossoms and leaves appear. In the gardens and in parks, flowers grow.

Summer starts on June 21. This is vacation season. It is hot. For city residents, the time has come to look for shade and relax in the country or the mountains or at the seashore. In the fields and gardens, crops and fruits are ripening. This is harvest time for such crops as oats and wheat. However, when the weather stays hot for a while, terrible storms often occur.

Autumn arrives on September 23. This is harvest season for the fruits that have ripened during the summer. But it is also the time when the leaves on trees turn yellow, red, and golden. Then they fall. The days become short. Cold sets in again, and the weather is frequently dull and rainy. The return of winter, which starts on December 22, is already being announced.

THE WATER

Like the earth, the planet Saturn (here photographed by the space probe Voyager II) revolves around the sun.

Where in space is the earth?

The earth, rotating around the sun, belongs to a solar system. Eight other planets are part of that system, too.

The sun is the largest body in this planetary system. Its volume is 330,000 times that of the earth. Earth is about 93 million miles (150 million km) from the sun. Other planets are located nearer to or farther from the sun.

Between the sun and the earth there are two planets. The closest one to the earth is Venus, followed by Mercury, which is next to the sun. Farther away from the earth are Mars, Jupiter, Saturn, Uranus, Neptune, and Pluto. Like the earth, these planets are satellites of the sun, and certain planets have satellites rotating around them. The moon is the earth's only satellite, but Jupiter has thirteen, and Saturn has twenty-three.

As you learned earlier, the earth is well positioned with respect to the sun. It is not too close for the heat to be unbearable, and not so far away that everything freezes.

What is between the sun and the earth?

There is void—no water, no air, no matter, an absolute void in which the stars and the planets orbit. In space, the temperature is extremely low, in the area of what is called absolute zero -460°F (-273°C).

The rays the sun sends into space move without hindrance. Nothing blocks their path except other planets or an occasional comet or another star. Nevertheless, the rays still lose a good part of their energy before they reach the earth. There is, however, still enough energy to warm the earth without burning it.

What is a good way to describe the earth?

The planet Venus, which is surrounded by opaque clouds, is called the white planet. Mars is the red planet because its surface has a red color. From space, the earth appears as a blue planet. The first astronauts who were launched in a rocket and orbited the earth at an altitude of several hundred miles saw it as a big blue ball.

This blue color stems from the oceans that cover the largest part of the earth and which are themselves blue. The continents take up little space compared to the seas. The Pacific Ocean, the Atlantic Ocean, the Indian Ocean, and the Arctic Ocean are much larger than the six continents that make up the solid earth—Asia, America, Africa, Antarctica, Europe, and Australia. About seventy percent of the terrestrial surface is covered with water. You will soon see that in meteorology, water, in all its forms, is the most important element of the weather.

This water stems from the origin of the earth. As the earth slowly cooled, it released immense quantities of water vapor around it. The water vapor came into contact with the very cold outer space and was transformed into clouds, then into rain. More than three billion years ago the seas were created in this manner. And in this water, life, from which humans have evolved, was created.

The earth (above and below) appears to be a blue planet. About seventy percent of its surface is covered by water. The continents are represented by the darker areas, and the cloudy masses look like white patches.

On the following double page—the solar system in its entirety. Observe the diversity of the planets' orbits.

17

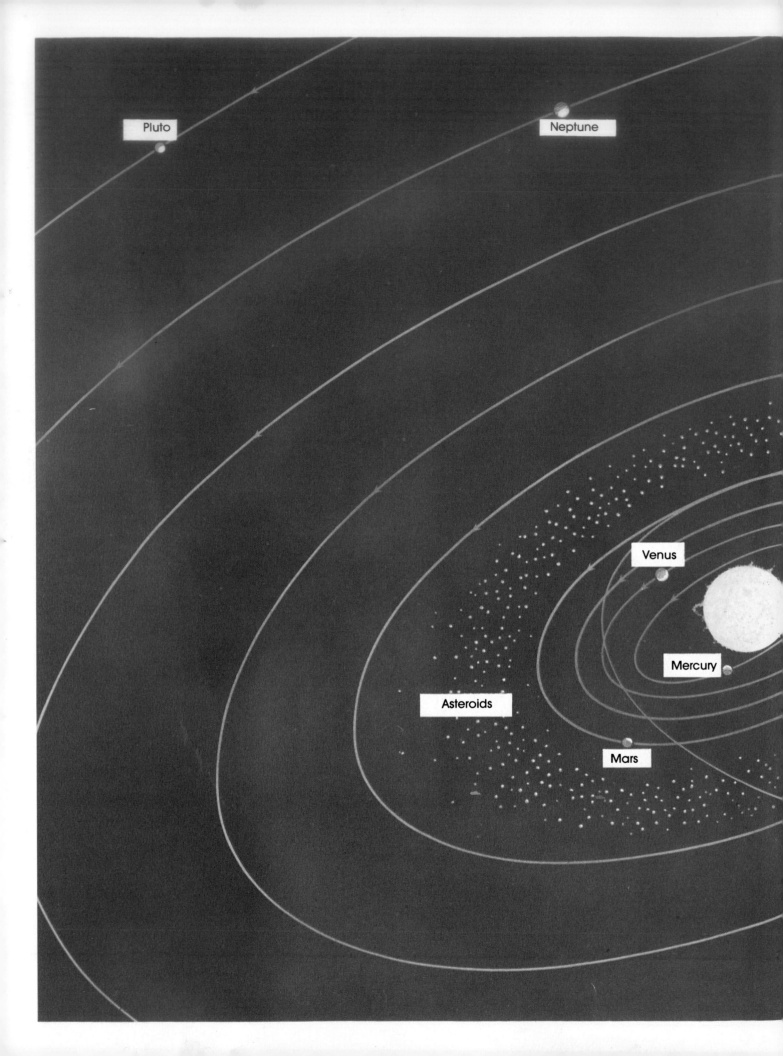

Uranus

Jupiter

Earth

Saturn

Halley's Comet

When the sun sets, its rays travel a long way in the atmosphere. The blue color is diffused in the sky, and red replaces it.

Why is the sky blue?

The rays of the sun, as they near the earth, meet the air particles that make up the upper layers of the atmosphere. There is an impact, and the rays are scattered. The white light of the sun, which consists of a mixture of seven colors (red, orange, yellow, green, blue, indigo, and violet), has its blue component scattered and reflected by the air. This colors the sky, and the process is called diffusion.

At sunset, the rays must travel a longer distance through the atmosphere. The blue color is completely diffused, and red appears. The same phenomenon occurs at sunrise.

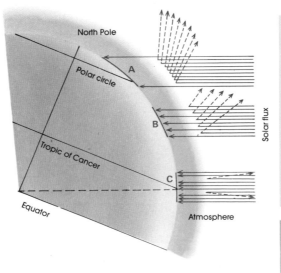

Solar rays do not reach the surface of the earth under the same condition at all points. In the areas closer to the poles, that is, in higher latitudes, the heat brought by solar rays is distributed on a surface that is much larger than at the equator.

Radiation

All physical objects give off radiation. The radiation has characteristics and an intensity that depend on the temperature of the body. A piece of ice, an animal, a person, the surface of the sea or that of the earth, all radiate. Except for very hot objects, the radiation is not visible. Special infrared film is required to see it.

Solar radiation

Solar radiation is composed of two parts. A visible part, white light, corresponds to a little less than half the radiation. The invisible part is almost totally filtered by the atmosphere. These are X-rays, cosmic rays, and ultraviolet rays.

Why does a street dry up after a rainfall?

In summer, a wet road can give off steam, then dry rapidly. Damp wash is hung on a line to dry. After a swim in the ocean, human bodies dry if they are in the sun. The water disappears. It has passed from the liquid state into the gaseous state. Water is transformed into water vapor. In other words, there has been evaporation.

The same happens to a pot of boiling water. The pan becomes empty quickly. Why? Because heat energy has been applied to the water. People need to dry themselves after a bath because their bodies supply heat to the drops of water adhering to their skin. If the drops evaporate, the body loses heat, causing a person to feel cold.

Water exists in three forms—solid (ice), liquid (water), and gas (vapor). Heating ice makes it melt and transforms it into water. Removing heat from the water in a refrigerator makes it freeze and transforms it into ice. Heating water makes it become vapor. Cooling vapor returns it to its liquid state.

The water that soaks laundry when it is being washed eventually transforms into vapor. It evaporates into the atmosphere. When the wind blows, drying takes place even faster.

THE WATER CYCLE

What is the water cycle?

Through its cycle, water seems to travel a merry-go-round. The sun shines upon the ocean. It gives off heat to the water. The water then passes to the gaseous state and evaporates. Vapor rises in the atmosphere. The greater the altitude the colder the atmosphere is.

Precipitation

Glacier

Torrent

Torrent

Evaporation

River

Infiltration of water into the ground

Flow of subterranean water

Consequently, the vapor cools down. It again becomes liquid. This is called condensation. At this instance it is important to note that when becoming water again, the vapor releases the heat it had used to become gas. It no longer needs this heat and gives it off to the surrounding air.

When it turns freezing cold outside, the temperature of liquid water cools down and reaches 32°F (0°C). The water turns to ice. This is the freezing point. Later on, the temperature rises and the ice warms up and melts, using some of the heat to become water again. This is called the heat of fusion.

Water never ceases to change form. The principal role of vapor is to transport heat from one place on the planet to another. The air surrounding the earth, thus, is a kind of bank that receives water in the form of vapor and returns it in the form of rain or snow. The quantities of water that have evaporated are equal to the quantities of water that fall to earth again.

In some very hot places, during the summer, the quantities of water that are transformed into vapor can be enormous. In the Gulf of Mexico, for example, the sun transforms 5 billion gallons (19 billion liters) of water per hour into vapor.

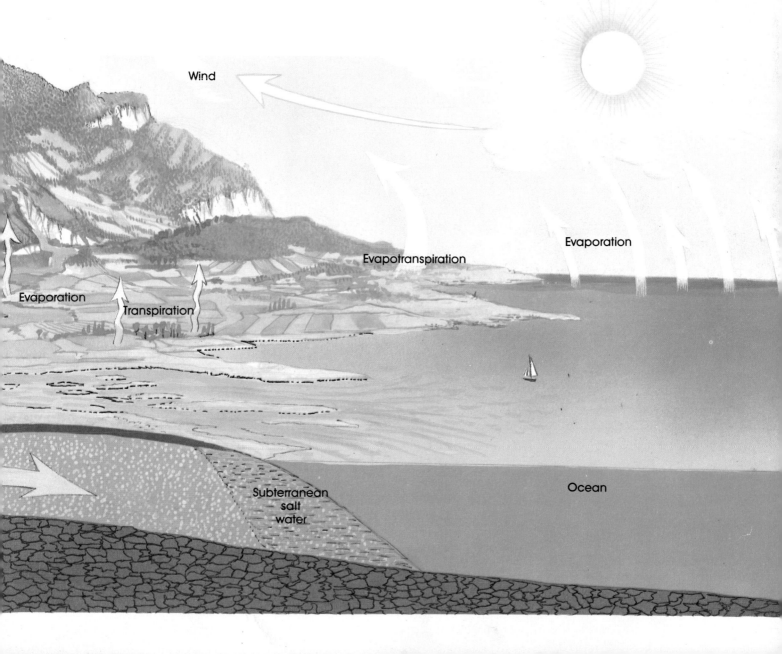

Why do clouds float in the sky?

Clouds are made of billions of miniscule water droplets with a lot of air between them. The air carries these droplets. They are composed of vapor that is cooled by rising in the atmosphere. It seems that clouds float. In reality, these droplets descend toward the earth due to gravity. But they are very light, and air rising from the earth is powerful enough to make the clouds "float" for a period of time.

Clouds form a barrier against the rays of the sun. At the top of a cloud, water droplets reflect light, and the cloud looks shiny and bright. But within the cloud, it is darker, since the sun's rays must cross a path that goes through the water droplets. This is difficult and when light succeeds in crossing the cloud, it has lost a great deal of its intensity.

If you have ridden in an airplane, you have without a doubt seen this magnificent spectacle—a "sea" of clouds.

Caution, fog! Everything is dim, and everything seems blurry. Car lights suddenly come into view.

Why is it hard to see in the fog?

It is hard to see in fog because fog is a cloud that forms at ground level or at sea level. For it to form, the temperature must be low. The cold air transforms water vapor into droplets. If winds don't disperse this forming cloud, there will be fog. It will dissipate when the sun's rays evaporate it.

In daytime, when it is hard to see in a fog, it is because the rays of the sun that enter from above collide with the water droplets in the fog. The bigger the droplets, the less that can be seen. Light is reflected in all directions. It is diffused, causing darkness.

This is why drivers turn on car headlights when there is fog. But even then it is hard to see since the light from the headlights is also diffused.

How much does a cloud weigh?

Clouds are composed of water droplets and water, both of which have weight. Of course, each droplet has an insignificant weight. But when they are all added together, the figures are impressive. The larger a cloud, the heavier it is. Some clouds are only several hundred feet wide and long, about the size of a hill. But others are larger than mountain chains.

A cloud with a side 1,600 feet (500 m) long and a height of 6,600 feet (2,000 m) weighs more than 1 billion pounds (500 million kilograms). This weight corresponds to an average of .105 ounce (3 grams) of water for 264 gallons (1,000 liters) of cloud.

Why do clouds move?

Clouds seem to float in the sky, like boats on a river or a lake. Just as there are water currents on earth, there are air currents in the sky. Clouds follow these currents. Movements of the air are simply called wind. Winds are created by temperature differences that exist on the surface of the earth.

As you know, warm air rises. When it does, it leaves a free space, a kind of hole in the space where it was. Immediately, air replaces that which has risen. This air could only be cold since, if it were hot, it would also rise.

Under these same circumstances, the sun heats the earth, and the earth reheats the air with which it is in contact. This air rises. It is at once replaced with colder air. The movement of one to the location of the other results in a wind. There are always places on earth where it is cold and places where it is warm. Therefore, there is always wind. Clouds follow the wind and go where the wind goes.

The air is in constant movement, creating wind. The clouds follow the wind.

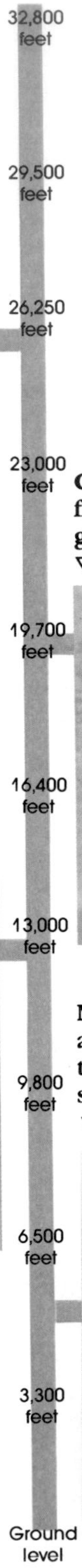

Cumulus: separated clouds with well-delineated contours and a horizontal base.

The Principal Types of Clouds

32,800 feet

29,500 feet

26,250 feet

23,000 feet

Cirrocumulus: small, globular masses of white, fleecy clouds arranged in ripple-like rows or groups.

19,700 feet

16,400 feet

13,000 feet

Cirrus: thin, detached, featherlike white clouds of ice.

Nimbostratus: continuous cloudy sheet, gray and often dark, the appearance of which is blurry through the more or less continuous rain or snowfall.

9,800 feet

6,500 feet

Altocumulus: fleecy cloud formation consisting of rounded heaps of white or grayish clouds, often partly shaded. Clouds with a large vertical expansion of 3,300 to 26,250 feet (1,000 to 8,000 m).

3,300 feet

Ground level

THE CLIMATES

What is the proper way to dress for winter?

At the North Pole

In polar regions, the sun's radiation passes above the pole. No solar rays mean no heat. The cold is extreme, down to -85°F (-65°C). Explorers of these regions must be covered from head to toe with thick furs. Eskimos live farther south. There it is a bit less cold, but furs are still absolutely necessary. The most effective "clothing" is to grease all parts of the body that are exposed to the cold. It prevents the skin from drying and preserves body heat.

For most people, the cold of winter is temporary. With the return of warmer days people leave their heavy coats behind. But for this young Eskimo (below), furs are an absolute necessity during most of the year.

At a distance from the poles

Elsewhere in the Northern Hemisphere it is also winter, but much less harsh than near the North Pole. In most places, a coat is indispensable, as well as thick socks, gloves, heavy pants, perhaps a pair of tights, scarfs, and hats. Wool is the warmest material for clothing. Some days are warmer, and a raincoat is sufficient covering.

In the Antilles

The Antilles are islands in the Caribbean Sea. Two of them are well known—Guadeloupe and Martinique. The weather of these countries is delightful. They experience winter, but it is mild. At noon on a typical day, it is between 79° and 84°F (26° and 29°C)! Thus, there is no need to dress warmly. The temperature of the water is at least 75°F (24°C).

January in Zaïre

Zaïre is a large African country in the Southern Hemisphere. During January, this region of the earth is exposed directly to the rays of the sun. That is why it is very hot. Just like in the Antilles, it is not necessary to dress warmly. But, since it rains frequently, people need raincoats.

In Australia

Australia is a huge island-nation in the Southern Hemisphere. It is an entire continent. Most of the country is desert. The Australians benefit from long summer days. Even if it rains, it is not very cold.

At the South Pole

The South Pole is almost entirely covered by ice—up to about 2 miles (3 km) thick. But, under this ice there is firm earth, the Antarctic continent. This is where the lowest temperature in the world has been recorded. In January, the South Pole is totally exposed to the sun. It remains daytime around the clock, but it is cold. In the sun, scientists who work there are comfortable wearing heavy clothing.

In January in Zaïre, there is sun and rain. Cars get stuck in the waterlogged ground.

A nice summer night 800 miles (1,300 km) from the South Pole! It is 23°F (-5°C)—very hot for 3 a.m. on February 6.

Why are climates so different?

The earth, with the exception of the equatorial regions, is never perpendicular to the rays of the sun, but at an angle with respect to them. At certain times, some areas are less inclined and receive more of the heat from the sun than other areas. These areas experience summer. In other regions, it is winter. The entire scope of changes in the weather in a given region during the course of a year is called the *climate*.

The seasons and the climates correspond to different amounts of heat and precipitation, depending on the time of year. It was noted earlier that because of the inclination of the earth, the sun seems to seesaw alternately from south to north, then from north to south, during an entire year. This is the apparent movement of the sun. Remember, however, it only appears this way. It is important to understand that a part of the earth is thus basked in abundant sunshine during almost the entire year. These are the regions located close to the equator.

On the other hand, those regions close to the poles are the coldest. In the Northern Hemisphere, hot air produced by the earth at the equator has the tendency to move toward the north, and cold air tends to move to the south. Inevitably, there are regions where the two air masses meet. These are the so-called temperate regions.

The United States and Europe are among them. The climate is not as warm as at the equator nor as cold as at the poles. In the Southern Hemisphere—Argentina, southern Australia, and New Zealand also belong to the temperate zones. Of course, there are exceptions to the rule.

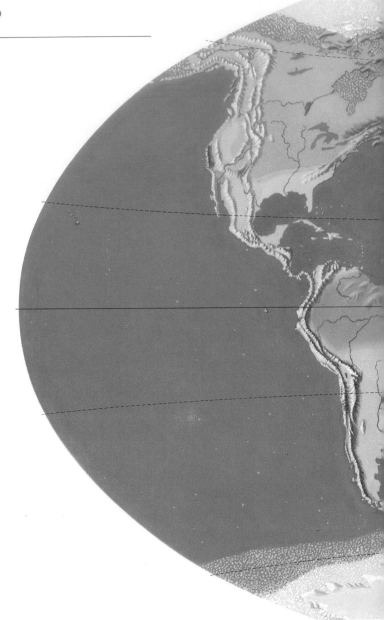

Where are humans located on the globe?

A long time ago, humans, particularly sailors, searched for a way to chart their location with respect to the places they knew. Thus, the method of taking a bearing was invented, with each place being at the intersection of two directions. With respect to the poles and the equator, two groups of circles have been developed. (1) Circles that are parallel to the equator, called parallels, number from 1 to 90 toward the poles. They permit the definition of latitude—the northern latitude between the equator and the North Pole, the southern latitude between the equator and the South Pole. (2) Circles passing through the poles, called meridians, number from 1 to 180 toward the east, and from 1 to 180 toward the west. They proceed from a prime meridian that passes near London, in Greenwich, England. Meridians define longitude. Each point of the globe can be represented by an intersection of a parallel and a meridian.

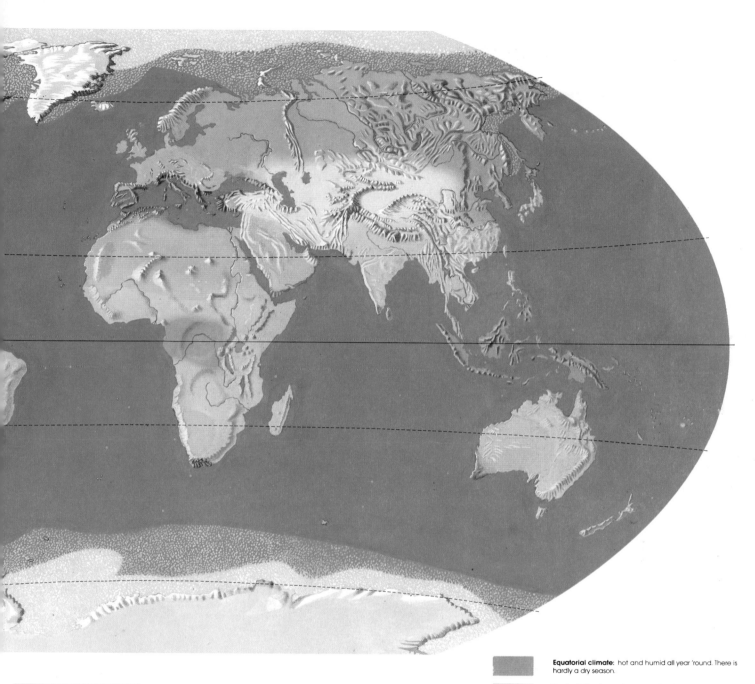

The sextant is used for measuring the angle of the sun or even a star above the horizon. Using the information obtained, a sailor calculates the position of his vessel.

The Main Types of Climates

Equatorial climate: hot and humid all year 'round. There is hardly a dry season.

Tropical climate: a rainy season that lasts on the average up to eight or ten months in the regions that are the farthest from the equator.

Subtropical climate: the few summer rainfalls are very irregular additions from one year to another.

Desert climate: hot all year 'round (Sahara, Australia); in summer, rains are exceptions. The temperatures are scorching.

Desert climate with cold winter and hot summer: temperatures can be very low in winter, but there is hardly any snow.

Mediterranean climate: long, dry summers; humid winters.

"Chinese" climate (in the southern part of China or southeastern United States): mild and dry winter; hot and humid summer.

Temperate maritime climate (on the western side of continents): humid, not very cold winters; cool and humid summers.

Temperate continental climate: long and cold winters, snowy; rather warm and rainy summers (thunderstorms).

Polar climate: very long winters (seven to eight months); very cold and dry, almost no snow; cool and dry short summers.

How is *climate* defined?

Pictured are ice in the polar regions, an oasis in a desert scorched by the sun, and trees in a temperate region. These three photos illustrate the diversity of landscapes with three different climates.

In each country, region, and town, the average characteristics of the season determine the climate. Climate can be defined on the basis of two things—temperature and precipitation (rain, snow, or hail).

A mountain region will not have the same climate as a plain. A valley situated on one side of the mountain does not necessarily have the same climate as another valley on the opposite side, even if the two are at the same altitude. A river, a lake, a marsh, or a forest can change the climate. A large city does not have the same climate as its suburbs because of the heat it gives off. Some countries are so big that they include almost all of the climates of the world in their boundaries.

There is no abrupt change in climate between two adjacent regions because the evolution of different types of weather happens gradually. In simple terms, each region, as small as it might be, will have its own climate. These multiple situations are called microclimates ("micro" meaning small).

What is a polar climate?

Greenland is a large island located northeast of North America. The largest part of its territory is continuously covered by ice. Winter lasts eight months, from October to May. It is a harsh environment. It never rains; it snows. Skis, dog-sleds, or snowshoes are used to move around. Moreover, the wind, which is a blizzard, is often extremely strong. When it blows, it is impossible to go outside. In winter, the sun hardly ever shines. When it does shine, it shines only from 10 a.m. to 2 p.m.

Summer arrives abruptly. It is almost nice weather. Ice melts on the riverbanks. Suddenly beautiful flowers shoot up, as well as moss and green grass. Flies and mosquitoes appear. Both will also leave quite suddenly at the beginning of the cold weather. Summer in Greenland lasts only four months, from June to September.

Icebergs break away from Greenland. These islands of ice are created on firm earth by the accumulation of snow and the thrusting of gigantic glaciers moving slowly toward the sea. As they move south, these icebergs melt. However, due to their size and hardness, they present a danger to ships. In 1912, the *Titanic,* a magnificent passenger liner, sank during its first crossing of the Atlantic, after having run into an iceberg.

In the Antarctic (top), bits of ice floes float on the sea. Impressive icebergs tower above them. In polar regions, even during the mild season, snow does not melt completely (right).

What is the best example of a temperate country?

France is an excellent example of a temperate climate. Without exception, it is never very hot or very cold. Obviously, once or twice a century, the weather doesn't follow its usual pattern. It becomes extremely hot or cold.

There are several reasons for a temperate climate. The first one is the geographical location of France, midway between the cold North Pole and the hot equator. Then there is the extensive contact of this country with the sea. A shoreline of 1,860 miles (3,000 km) is significant. The influence of the Atlantic Ocean can be felt far into the interior of the country, even more so since few mountains stop it. The resulting humidity from the sea conserves heat in winter or moderates excessive heat in summer. The sea mellows the climate and brings rain. It rains throughout the year, moderately but regularly, which is what allows France to be a great agricultural country. The climate is thus temperate, but one can still distinguish between four types of seasons—winter is cold, but not too cold; spring is quite mild; summer is pleasantly warm; fall is fresh.

Other elements reinforce this moderation of the French climate. The country is at a junction of multiple climates. When the air comes from the north, it is cool or cold. If the weather comes from the west, it is mild and humid. If it comes from the east, it is nice and dry without clouds. Finally, air from the south is heavy with heat and thunderstorms. During the entire year, the weather comes from these four directions successively. It is quite rare that the same type of weather persists for a long time. Thus, on the whole, the most frequent weather comes from the west, the Atlantic Ocean, bringing along clouds, rain, and wind, but also mildness. It is said that France is under a western influence. Naturally, the same amounts of rain do not fall everywhere, and it seldom rains everywhere at the same time. Snow is more abundant and frequent in the north or the east. This variety creates a sort of mosaic of micro-climates, but none of them are extreme.

France is just one example of a temperate climate.

Oceanic influences profoundly mark the general climate of France. Gentle, humid winds coming from the west make for a typically temperate climate.

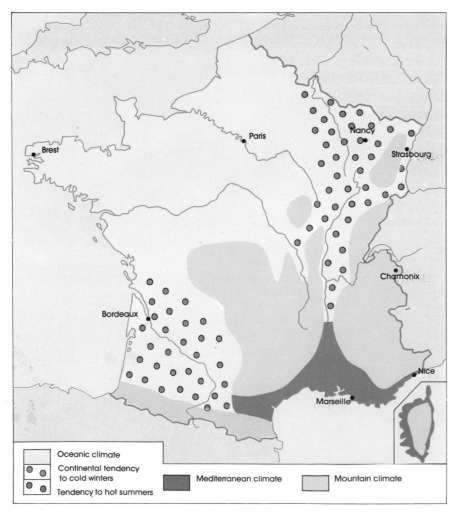

Oceanic climate

Continental tendency to cold winters

Tendency to hot summers

Mediterranean climate

Mountain climate

Above is Ajaccio, a typical Mediterranean port. In the Mediterranean are hills covered with maquis (underbrush) and grapevines (below).

Is a Mediterranean climate limited to the Mediterranean?

No, the Mediterranean climate does not just surround the area of the Mediterranean Sea. This name is used for a particular type of climate. Parts of South Africa, California, Chile, and Australia also have Mediterranean climates.

The symbol of this climate is the grapevine. It originated in the Mediterranean before being introduced further north or to the entire world. Vines require water at certain times in their lives. At other times they need sun. The Mediterranean climate is perfect for this. Such is also the case with the olive tree.

Temperatures are mild throughout the year. It is not too cold during the dry winter. In spring, rain storms that are often violent and abundant allow the vegetation to grow profusely. Summer is hot and dry. It is the season of devastating forest fires. Fall is rainy and moderate.

What is a subtropical climate?

The Sahara is a vast desert in the heart of Africa. It extends over thousands of miles in length and width, covering several countries. The Sahara is home to groups of nomads still traveling on camelback in caravans. It hardly ever rains there, and the heat is often unbearable because there is no humidity to temper the weather. The air is, therefore, very dry. Trees can only grow at infrequently found oases.

The temperature in the Sahara is very, very hot, up to 136°F (58°C), a record heat never exceeded in the world. But at night, since there is no water to retain the heat, it is cold. It even freezes, and stones will burst. They were heated during the day and expanded. When brisk cold arrives, they contract and explode. The Sahara also has storms—sandstorms.

This climate is called subtropical continental. Plenty of water would convert these regions into a paradise. But only in the oases is there water, or in some valleys such as the Nile in Egypt, which was the origin of a magnificent civilization.

Amidst the sand and rocks, water turns the Sahara into an oasis.

What is a tropical climate?

The Antilles are located near the Tropic of Cancer. They are islands. Some of them are very large. Others, such as Guadeloupe, Martinique, and Barbados are small. It is hot all year long, during the day as well as the night. The days when the sun does not shine are rare. It also rains a lot—frequently, violently, but briefly.

The vegetation is exquisite. The area is beautifully forested. From January to May, the air is relatively dry. It rains very little, and it is hot. June to December is the winter season. But this does not mean that it is cold. On the contrary, it is hot and sultry. The end of August, September, and the beginning of October constitute a kind of rainy season. It rains a lot, but the sun shines frequently. This is the time when dreadful and extremely violent storms arise, causing considerable damage.

A tropical maritime climate has summer all year long and a warm sea lined with coconut palms. The Antilles are influenced by regular winds always coming from the same direction. These winds, called the trade winds, make the temperatures milder.

Under the hot sun of the tropics are the Antilles (above). It is on one of these islands that Christopher Columbus landed in the New World in 1492. Below is a reconstruction of the ship in which Columbus sailed.

Where can an equatorial climate be found?

In the equatorial forest, only the rivers create a passage in the extremely dense vegetation.

Equatorial Africa, parts of which include the equator, is a good example of an equatorial climate. Cameroon, Gabon, and Zaïre are some nations in this region where the rays of the sun hit almost directly onto the surface of the land and sea. In these regions, evaporation is considerable. In equatorial Africa, there are always clouds all year-around.

As far as temperatures are concerned, the equatorial climate is not different from the tropical maritime climate. It is hot throughout the year. However, the rains are different. There are two distinct periods —one when it hardly rains, and one when it rains too much. These are called the dry season and the rainy season. This is why there is practically no rainfall in December and January, and from June to August. During the other months, it pours for days, even several weeks in a row. Each year in equatorial Africa 79 to 118 inches (2 to 3 m) of rain fall, which is enormous. But even when it rains, it is not cold.

THE UNPREDICTABLE WEATHER

In the polluted air of big cities, the fog sometimes becomes incredibly thick. In London, the well-known smog hinders traffic.

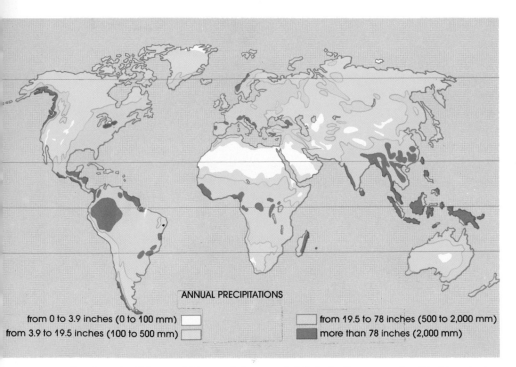

ANNUAL PRECIPITATIONS

from 0 to 3.9 inches (0 to 100 mm) ☐

from 3.9 to 19.5 inches (100 to 500 mm) ☐

from 19.5 to 78 inches (500 to 2,000 mm) ☐

more than 78 inches (2,000 mm) ☐

Some parts of the world have minimum rainfall, but others are submitted to genuine deluges. This map of annual precipitation shows tremendous differences around the world.

How is rain formed?

Rain is the result of evaporation. The heat from the sun transforms water into water vapor, that is, into gas. Lighter than air, it rises in the atmosphere. But the higher it goes, the colder it gets. The water vapor condenses and turns into miniscule droplets that form a cloud. These tiny little drops have a diameter of 0.0008 inches (1/50 of a millimeter). They are so light that they stay in the air.

It is then that condensation nuclei come into play. These are small, solid particles—dust, salt crystals from the ocean, and debris from factory smoke. They are smaller than the water droplets. In one cubic inch of pure air there are several thousands of these miniscule bodies. Above an industrial town, where the air is very dense with these particles, the condensation nuclei are counted by the millions per cubic inch or centimeter. Around these nuclei, the droplets enlarge. Others unite with them, brought in by the wind. The largest droplets absorb the smallest ones. When the diameter of the drops reaches an average of 0.02 inches (0.5 mm), rain is created. The weight is sufficient to make the drops fall. It rains. When there are only small drops, the rain is a drizzle of fine rain. During a thunderstorm, the diameter of the drops can reach 0.2 inches (5 mm).

Finally, when fog develops in the vicinity of a city very polluted by factories, such as Los Angeles or London, smog results. This is a mixture of air, of droplets, and pollution of all kinds.

Where does a rainbow get its colors?

Sunlight, diffracted by water drops, lets all colors of the rainbow appear (above). Just like rain, a waterfall can furnish the curtain of droplets necessary for a rainbow (right).

A rainbow is the result of the diffraction of sunlight through drops of water suspended in the atmosphere. Each ray from the sun is composed of several components, each having a specific color—red, orange, yellow, green, blue, indigo, and violet. When a ray strikes a raindrop, it is submitted to reflections and refractions, that is, it is dispersed, separated, and divided by the drop. Thus, the individual colors appear. To have a rainbow, sun and rain are needed. This is the type of weather that comes with sudden showers. If the drops are big, the color red will be more noticeable. If they are small, green will be prominent. Sometimes a second rainbow, inversed, surrounds the first.

Is it raining or snowing?

Snow is rain in its solid state. It forms in the cold regions of clouds. Water droplets transform themselves into ice crystals of great beauty. If the ground is warm, the snow will melt immediately. It "sticks" when the earth is cold.

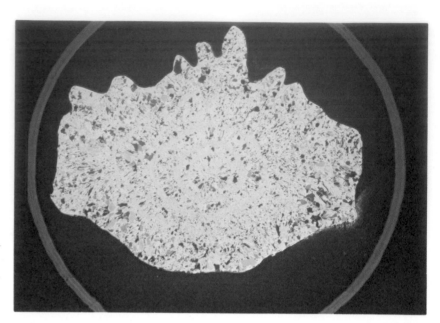

A section of a hailstone seen under a microscope.

Snow is rain in a solid state.

Why does hail cause damage?

Hail has ruined this cornfield.

Rain forms inside of clouds. But if the temperataure of the cloud is much below zero, the water droplets transform into ice and can, in certain cases, produce hail.

Hail is created in large clouds called cumulonimbus. Here there exist strong, vertical currents. Water droplets freeze and descend. But the current makes them rise again, then fall again, then rise again while getting larger and freezing, melting, freezing, and so on. Ice is formed in several layers. When its weight is heavier than the ascending currents, hail falls. Each ball of ice is called a hailstone. Some of them can be very big. In the United States, some have been found that weighed 0.7 pounds (300 grams). It is not surprising that they can break windows, dent cars, and destroy vegetation. On the average, a hailstone measures 0.02 inches (.5 mm) in diameter.

Hail does not only exist in cold countries. Once in a while, it even falls in the tropics.

Why does a thunderstorm occur?

The sky suddenly darkens. Thick black clouds have rapidly hidden the sun, as if night has fallen suddenly. A thunderstorm is about to occur.

Thunderstorms are violent aspects of the weather that are accompanied by lightning, thunder, and often abundant rainfall or hail. Storms usually start out on the inside of the gigantic cumulonimbus clouds.

In these clouds, powerful vertical air currents rise and descend. Large raindrops form and sometimes hail, and an imbalance exists between the positive and negative electrical charges of the cloud.

At the time of a storm, the top of a cumulonimbus cloud is positively charged and the base is negatively charged, like a battery. On the outside of the cloud, an unbalanced state also exists between the negative base of the cloud and the positive ground, or the positive base and the negative ground. At the moment when positive and negative regions encounter each other, an electrical discharge is produced and lightning strikes.

Why does a thunderstorm make so much noise?

In the course of a thunderstorm when lightning develops, it is accompanied by a loud noise called thunder. Thunder can be heard up to 15.5 miles (25 km) from its point of origin. The atmosphere is shattered by the lightning. The air is jolted, and this jolt creates a great noise.

The shattering noise travels at the speed of sound or 1,115 feet (340 m) per second. It is easy to calculate the distance to the point where the lightning is produced by counting the number of elapsed seconds between the sight of lightning and the arrival of the thunder. Then multiply the obtained number by 1,115 feet (340 m).

43

Where does lightning originate?

A lightning bolt is a bright, wavy beam of light, striking from a thundercloud toward the ground, from between two clouds, or from a cloud toward the sky. It is the consequence of electrical imbalance. A discharge is thus produced by the lightning, reestablishing the equilibrium.

A flash of lightning can reach up to 9 miles (15 km) in length. It can be seen as soon as it is produced because light emitted by it moves at 186,000 miles (300,000 km) per second. A bolt of lightning is short but violent. That is why it is dangerous. If someone is struck by lightning, that person is often in danger of burning to death.

To provide protection from bolts of lightning, the lightning rod was invented. Located in a high place, it is a metal rod (metal conducts electricity well) that intercepts the electrical energy and conducts it into the ground where it dissipates.

Lightning bolts crisscross the cloud-filled sky. Thunder rumbles and growls. The storm's violence crashes down on the town, accompanied by heavy downpours.

What is a storm?

A storm is a large whirl of clouds accompanied by rain and wind plus waves on the sea. A storm is born out of the shock produced by different air masses colliding: a warm one and a cold one. The more the temperatures contrast, the more violent the storm. Generally, a storm is characterized by a drastic drop in pressure. Following the drop in pressure, there are continuous rains and an overcast sky. Afterward, the weather varies, sun and clouds play hide-and-seek, and showers continue. In the United States, winds blow from the southwest before the bulk of the storm and from the northwest afterward.

The size of a storm varies. On the average, though, a storm measures 1,240 to 2,480 miles (2,000 to 4,000 km) from north to south and 372 to 2,480 miles (600 to 4,000 km) from east to west. This can be seen on photos taken by satellites.

Heavy winds create waves. Rain, wind, and waves cause considerable damage. When there are large storms, there are often deaths at sea and on land.

A storm along the coast. Seawater bursts and flattens out the piers that border the ocean. On the sea, ships unable to find shelter in time fight against the unleashed elements.

Following double page: A ship on the high seas.

This tornado was photographed in Oklahoma. Between the cloud and the ground, a kind of funnel eats up dust. An extremely strong wind sweeps everything in its path.

What is a tornado?

A tornado is a storm that concentrates a great amount of energy into a small space. It resembles a funnel that connects the ground to the cloud and eats up everything in its path. The winds inside sometimes rotate at more than 186 miles (300 km) per hour. Fortunately, tornadoes last only for a few hours. The damage they cause, however, is considerable, especially in the United States where they often occur in summer. Generally, tornadoes are accompanied by hail and heavy rain. They measure at most only a few hundred yards in length and width. They are very visible, which makes them easy to spot and to follow.

What is a monsoon?

A monsoon is a very particular phenomenon. The most famous example is that of India.

During the summer, in the Northern Hemisphere, the huge mainland regions located north of the Himalayas become overheated. The air rises and is replaced by air originating in the Southern Hemisphere. This air has traveled on warm seas and is saturated with water. It warms up even more above India and causes abundant rain. When this warm, moist air arrives at the mountainous regions of the Himalayas, more than 32 feet (10 m) of rain falls in some valleys. Flooding is rampant.

During winter, on the contrary, in the Northern Hemisphere, the mainland is relatively cold. The Indian Ocean in the Southern Hemisphere is warm. The wind blows from the regions of India toward the Southern Hemisphere. It is dry at the outset and becomes saturated with water while warming up above the ocean. Then it rains on Madagascar and on Reunion (islands in the Indian Ocean).

The monsoon is an excellent example of air exchanges that take place between the two hemispheres of the earth. Meteorologists consider the atmosphere as a whole because meteorological phenomena can be understood only on a global level.

Countries that are subjected to the monsoon have two principal seasons—a dry season in winter and a rainy season in summer. For India, the monsoon is indispensable for raising crops. However, in some years there is too much rain. This causes floods and damage. The monsoon is also sometimes associated with violent tropical cyclones. In other years there is not enough rain. A cycle of drought and famine then brings starvation to thousands of people.

The monsoon is not only Indian. Other regions in the world experience this type of climate, especially West Africa and Australia, but to a lesser degree.

In India, the overcast sky with heavy clouds announces the monsoon rains. For regions that are subjected to long, dry periods, this water is a blessing. However, it sometimes falls in such large quantities that it causes catastrophic floods.

49

A blizzard is a violent and icy wind that brings snow. Here, on the Antarctic continent, it surrounds vehicles on a polar excursion. Imagine the early explorers who had only simple tents to protect themselves.

What is a blizzard?

Blizzard is the name given to a wind coming from the north over Canada, Alaska, Russia, and Siberia. This cold, intense wind causes snowstorms that can be compared to the intensity of sandstorms. It is impossible to go out during a blizzard.

A blizzard occurs when a mass of cold air moves out of the Arctic into the temperate zone. The cold air forces the warm air to rise along the point between the two air masses. The rising action produces a heavy snowstorm with cold, north winds.

What is a cyclone?

A cyclone is a low-pressure area in the atmosphere where winds spiral inward. A cyclone can be so huge that it covers an area half as big as the United States.

The winds blow counterclockwise in the Northern Hemisphere. They blow clockwise in the Southern Hemisphere.

A tropical cyclone is called a hurricane in the West Indies or a typhoon in the Pacific Ocean. These storms can have winds up to 180 miles (290 km) per hour.

THE WEATHER

How is meteorological information obtained?

To foresee weather is not easy, although that is the daily work of meteorologists. Each day they obtain basic information and use these facts to predict the weather.

On all the continents, in thousands of research stations, meteorologists observe the sky. They measure the temperature, the pressure, the force and direction of the wind, and the humidity on the surface and at various altitudes. The same measurements are conducted on ships and in airplanes. Other meteorologists work with radar or send up weather balloons to analyze the atmosphere. Finally, satellites that produce pictures of the clouds below are an excellent supplement for information gathering.

To be useful, data must be transmitted. For this purpose, meteorologists use a global code to transmit their readings as quickly as possible.

In each country, national observations are consolidated and sent to a station responsible for a continent or a group of countries. Then each region sends the information to other regions.

The meteorological station of Mao, in the north of Chad in Africa, was established in 1953. What a difference there is between this shelter and the ones constructed today!

In the station of Entebbe, Uganda, a meteorologist regulates a heliograph. This device measures the duration of insolation, that is, the time during which the sun has shone.

An example

It is 5:50 a.m. in Nguimi, Nigeria. A meteorologist carries out an observation, codes it, and phones it to Zinder, another city in Nigeria. At 6:10 a.m., Zinder consolidates the information from this eastern region of Nigeria and sends it to Niamey, the capital. At 6:15 a.m., Niamey has received all the readings from Nigeria. Five minutes later, the observations of the neighboring country, Upper Volta, arrive. At 6:30 a.m., Niamey transmits the data from Nigeria and Upper Volta to Senegal. At Dakar, the capital of Senegal, meteorologists consolidate the information from West Africa. They send it to Paris by satellite at 6:40 a.m. At 7:30 a.m., the observation from Nguimi is available in Washington, D.C., Moscow, or Melbourne. The entire world has received it.

The entire world receives this information because all of this information is worthwhile in meteorology. The weather of one country is not isolated. Meteorological phenomena are all connected with each other in a chain.

How is meteorological information used?

Preceding page:
Ground stations, buoys and vessels, radar, airplanes, satellites, balloons, rockets—meteorologists have at their disposal the most modern means to study the atmosphere to make accurate weather predictions.

Connected to computers, the tracing table (below left) permits the automatic reporting of information received from all over the world onto maps. To the right is an information room where these data are stored and analyzed by powerful computers.

To understand the development of the weather, forecasters analyze meteorological information. Cloudy zones, rain, winds, storms, perfect calm, cyclones, all must be placed on a map. Meteorologists note the temperature of the air on the surface and at different altitudes, the temperature of the sea, and warm and cold air masses. By comparing new maps with preceding maps, they can determine the shift of storms or nice weather, the movement of the winds, and the rise and fall of temperature or pressure. No storm is exactly like any other. Everything moves on the surface of the globe within a layer of air that surrounds it. These air movements are not completely understood. After the analysis, the forecast, as it is properly called, is generated.

The laws of air movement in the atmosphere, the experience of the meteorologists, what is known about climates, all of this information generally allows for a good short-term forecast. Furthermore, the work to-day is aided by powerful computers. These computers analyze millions of bits of data each day. This data is then interpreted by the meteorologists. Thanks to computers, meteorologists can predict the weather from twelve to seventy-two hours in advance with a good chance of accuracy.

Some computers, more powerful than others, attempt predictions for up to ten days.

These predictions are not very accurate, since the majority of phenomena in the atmosphere are on a tremendous scale. A cyclone, for example, generates the energy equivalent of four to five nuclear bombs each second. These types of phenomena are still too overwhelming to be incorporated into daily weather predictions.

Knowledge of international occurrences is improved by having the entire world combine its wealth of knowledge. By the year 2000, meteorologists will be able to make very accurate long-term predictions.

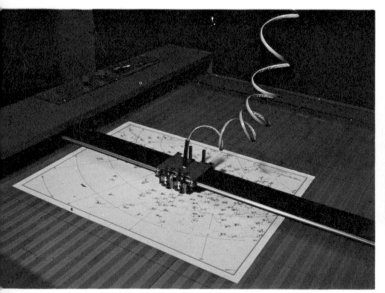

Of what use is a weather report?

The weather affects everybody. What should you wear today? Is it necessary to take an umbrella or a coat before leaving for work? These are simple but important questions in everyday living.

But there are more serious questions. It is imperative that the farmer, awaiting the ideal moment for the harvest or for preventing frost on fruit trees, takes notice of the weather report.

The airplane pilot embarking on a long trip wants to know the weather ahead in order to avoid storms and to make use of high-altitude winds that will help him or her arrive earlier and save fuel. The captain of a ship can avoid entering a cyclone, where the vessel might be lost. The weather report gives the captain the location of the phenomenon. The police must know which roads are coated with ice or are snowed in, in order to warn drivers or to order sanding.

The science of meteorology has existed since 1860. It is an international science serving everyone around the world.

In the mountains, avalanches cause accidents each year. Luckily, meteorologists have often managed to warn people of this danger. They are not always sure about the exact angle of descent, but they know whether there is a risk involved.

No airline pilot takes off without knowing the atmospheric conditions to be encountered during the flight. The pilot must take into account information from the weather report in order to choose the best course.

Can anyone be a meteorologist?

Humans have always observed the sky. They have tried to penetrate its secrets and to define its laws.

Farmers who live in contact with nature on a daily basis often know what kind of weather they are about to experience without listening to a weather forecast. They know how to interpret the shape and height of clouds, the direction and force of the wind, and the behavior of certain animals.

Observant people can make amateur, but accurate, predictions by carefully watching the development of the weather.

Of course, in order to become a professional meteorologist, a person must attend college to study this specialized field.

Agriculture schools often have such meteorological instruments as a rain gauge.

The anemometer measures wind speed.

Why are there errors in weather predictions?

If errors are made, it is because humans do not yet know everything about the atmosphere and its movements. Meteorology is a young science in need of a lot of research and time in order to be perfected. Considerable progress has been made regarding an understanding of the weather, and more will come in future years. With it will come better predictions.

A meteorological shelter is reflected in the heliograph ball, an apparatus that measures the length of solar radiation.

Next page:
Carried by a balloon, a radio probe measures the pressure, the temperature, and the humidity up to an altitude of 19 miles (30 km). The small parachute near the top will prevent a damaging fall of the apparatus, but an accident is always possible. For example, the balloon might burst.

A balloon carrying a radiosonde.

Can pollution change the weather?

Carbon dioxide is not a good gas for humans and animals to breathe. But plants and trees absorb carbon dioxide in the atmosphere and produce oxygen in return. This is an important service because oxygen is indispensable. Without oxygen, humans and animals would die of suffocation. But all around the world, people are cutting down the forests. They are destroying a reservoir of oxygen. This, too, is pollution of the atmosphere because oxygen is being diminished.

The entire earth needs oil. Sometimes an oil-carrying vessel sinks, and its cargo spills into the ocean. Captains of ships even dare to clean their tanks on the high sea and return the polluted waters to the ocean. Little by little, all the oceans of the world could become covered by a very thin film of oil, which would act like a screen between the water and the sun. Were that to continue, water evaporation would diminish. There would be fewer clouds, thus less rain. Agriculture would suffer, droughts would be common, the lives of millions would be at stake. This is why scientists specifically study the problems connected with the pollution of the surface of the oceans.

A polluted view of a portion of the New York skyline.

Next page: Los Angeles is one of the most polluted cities in the world.

The smoke from factories, as it is pulled down by winds, pollutes numerous industrial cities.

Can people change the weather?

This anti-hail cannon was invented at the beginning of the twentieth century.

A religious procession asking the heavens to watch over the crops.

It is an old dream of humans to control the weather, to be able to make it rain when there is drought or to stop the rain in case of floods. Humans have tried and are still trying to change the weather without a great deal of success.

Hail causes enormous damage. Some experimenters, when seeing a cloud approach and suspecting a hail shower, shoot rockets into them, either from the ground or from a plane, in order to transform the hail into rain. The results are not convincing. Attempts have also been made to make rain by injecting particles into clouds that will adhere to the water droplets to artificially produce raindrops. Here again, the results have not been outstanding. Furthermore, do humans have the right to cause rain? The quantity of water contained in a cloud is not unlimited. To make rain fall in one area, is that not stealing from regions where it should have fallen? Who is to decide where rain will do the most good?

Attempts have also been made to suppress cyclones. A project called Stormfury aims to diminish the intensity of hurricanes by means of a very complicated system for modifying the eye of the cyclone. But it appears that cyclones will remain a part of nature's arsenal.

Glossary

atmosphere   a gaseous mass surrounding a planet or other celestial body; especially, the mass of air enveloping the earth.

climate   the average course or condition of weather at a specific place over a long period of time. Climate is defined mainly by temperature and precipitation.

condensation   the process of water vapor changing to a liquid state.

condensation nuclei   the tiny particles of matter on which water vapor condenses.

diffraction   the spreading of light waves around an opaque object.

diffusion   the reflection of light from a rough surface such as a piece of paper. When light is diffused, it scatters or spreads out.

equator   the imaginary line running around the earth exactly halfway between the North Pole and the South Pole. The equator marks 0° latitude.

equinox   one of two days of the year when the sun is directly above the equator. During an equinox, the length of daylight and darkness is nearly equal everywhere on earth. The spring equinox takes place on March 21. September 21 marks the autumn equinox.

evaporation   the process of converting a liquid to a vapor.

fog   a cloud with its base at or very near the ground.

freezing point   the temperature at which a liquid becomes a solid. The freezing point of water is 32° Fahrenheit or 0° Celsius.

hurricane   a tropical cyclone with winds reaching 186 miles (300 km) per hour, usually accompanied by rain, thunder, and lightning. Hurricanes are among the greatest storms on earth.

latitude   refers to the imaginary lines that run from east to west around the earth. Latitude is measured in degrees with the equator being 0°. Lines of north latitude are found above the equator and measure from 0° to 90°. Those below the equator are lines of south latitude. These also measure from 0° to 90°.

longitude   refers to the imaginary lines that run from the North Pole to the South Pole. Longitude is measured in degrees starting with a line at 0° running through Greenwich, England. This is called the prime meridian. Lines east of this line are called east longitude. Those west of it are known as west longitude. Both go halfway around the earth and meet directly opposite the prime meridian at 180° longitude.

meridian   one of the imaginary circles on the earth's surface that passes through the North and South poles, marking longitude.

microclimate   the essentially uniform climate found in a small site or location.

monsoon   the periodic wind that affects the climates of large areas and reverses direction seasonally. Countries affected by monsoons have two principal seasons: a dry season in winter, and a rainy season in summer.

oasis   a fertile, green area in an arid region.

parallel   one of the imaginary circles of the earth's surface running parallel to the equator and marking latitude.

precipitation   water droplets or ice crystals that fall to earth as rain, snow, hail, sleet, or glaze.

prime meridian   the meridian of 0° longitude which passes through Greenwich, England. East and west longitude are measured from this point.

reflection   the return of light or sound waves from a surface. Light waves reflected from a smooth surface bounce back without spreading out. Waves reflected from a rough surface, however, spread out or diffuse.

refraction   the bending of a wave, such as light or sound, as it passes from one substance into another. Refraction of light, for example, occurs when light passes through glass or water.

satellite (artificial) an object or vehicle made on earth which is intended to orbit the earth, the moon, or other celestial body. Artificial satellites are often used to study the weather.

satellite (natural) planets or other bodies that circle around another celestial body of a larger size. The planets in the solar system are satellites of the sun; the moon is the earth's satellite.

sextant an instrument used in navigation for measuring the altitude between the plane of the horizon and celestial bodies.

solar flare a sudden and temporary outburst of gases from a small area of the sun's surface.

solstice one of two days of the year on which the sun appears at its farthest point north or south among the stars. The solstice represents the longest and shortest day (length of daylight) of the year. In the Northern Hemisphere, the summer solstice falls on June 21. The winter solstice is on December 21. These solstices are reversed in the Southern Hemisphere.

tornado a local, violent storm made of whirling winds rotating around a central cavity. Tornadoes, often called twisters or cyclones, last only a short time but are among nature's most destructive forces.

trade wind an extremely consistent wind found in the tropics, which blows almost continually toward the equator.

typhoon a tropical cyclone occurring in the west Pacific Ocean or the China Sea.

visible spectrum the rainbow-like band of colors contained in white light. The spectrum consists of all the light waves that the eye can see. They appear as colors because the eye sees the different wave lengths as different colors. These colors include: red, orange, yellow, green, blue, indigo, and violet.

water cycle the never-ending movement of the earth's water from the oceans, to the air, to the land, and back to the oceans again.

weather the state of the atmosphere at a particular place for a short period of time.

wind the movement of air masses. Winds are named for the direction *from* which they blow.

INDEX

air currents, 25, 42
air pressure, 45, 50
altocumulus (cloud), 26
annual rainfall, 40
anti-hail cannon, 61
asteroid, 18
atmosphere, 11, 20, 59
autumn, 14
autumn equinox, 10, 14
avalanche, 55
blizzard, 33, 50
blue planet, 17
carbon dioxide, 59
"Chinese" climate, 31
chromosphere, 11
cirrocumulus (cloud), 26
cirrus (cloud), 26
climate, 27-38
    factors of , 32
clouds, 24-26
    types of, 26
color spectrum, 20, 41
condensation, 23
condensation nuclei, 40, 61
cosmic rays, 20
cumulonimbus (cloud), 42, 43
cumulus (cloud), 26
cyclone, 49, 50, 54, 61
desert climate, 31
diffraction, 41
diffusion, 20
dry season, 38, 49
duration of insolation, 52
earth, 19
    revolution, 12-14
    rotation, 12-14
    orbit, 13
electrical charge, 43
electrical imbalance, 43-44
equator, 20, 30
equatorial climate, 31, 38
equatorial forest, 38
evaporation, 21-23, 40, 59
evapotranspiration, 23
flood, 49
fog, 24, 40
forecaster, 54
freezing point, 23
funnel, 48
glacier, 33
gravity, 24

Greenwich (England), 30
hail (hailstone), 42, 61
Halley's Comet, 19
heat of fusion, 23
heliograph, 52, 57
hurricane, 50, 61
ice crystal, 42
ice floe, 33
iceberg, 33
Jupiter, 16, 19
latitude, 20, 30
lightning, 43, 44
lightning rod, 44
longitude, 30
maquis, 35
Mars, 16, 17, 18
Mediterranean climate, 31,
    34, 35
Mercury, 16, 18
meridian, 30
meteorological observations,
    52-55
meteorological station, 52
meteorology, 17, 55, 57
microclimate, 32
monsoon, 49
moon, 16
mountain climate, 34
Neptune, 16, 18
nimbostratus (cloud), 26
oasis, 36
oceanic climate, 34
parallel, 30
planets, 16-19
Pluto, 16, 18
polar axis, 12, 13
polar circle, 20
polar climate, 31, 33
pollution, 40, 59
precipitation (*see also* rain,
    hail, snow), 22
prime meridian, 30
radar, 52, 45
radiation, 20
radio probe, 57
rain, 40
    annual amounts of, 40
rainbow, 41
rainy season, 38, 49
reflection, 20, 41
refraction, 41

rockets, 54, 61
sandstorm, 36
satellite (artificial), 12, 45, 52, 54
satellite (natural), 16
Saturn, 16, 19
seasons, 7-14, 30
sextant, 31
snow, 42
solar eclipse, 11
solar flare, 11
solar flux, 20
solar rays, 11, 13, 16, 20, 24
solar system, 16-19
speed of sound, 43
spring, 14
spring equinox, 10, 14
storm, 45
    size, 45
Stormfury, 61
subtropical climate, 31, 36
summer, 10, 14
summer solstice, 10, 13, 14
sun, 10-13
temperate climate, 34
temperate maritime climate, 31
thunder, 43, 44
thunderstorm, 43
Titanic, 33
tornado, 48
trade winds, 37
transpiration, 23
Tropic of Cancer, 20, 37
tropical climate, 31, 37
tropical maritime climate, 38
tropics, 9
typhoon, 50
Uranus, 16, 19
Venus, 16, 17, 18
water, 16-26
    currents, 25
    cycle, 21-23
    forms of, 21
weather balloon, 52-54
weather map, 54
white light, 20
wind, 45, 48, 50
    origin of, 25
winter, 8-9, 14, 28
winter solstice, 10, 13, 14